Virtual Reality in Nanotechnology

A Journey into the Minuscule World

Table of Contents

Chapter 1. Introduction

In this Special Report, we will delve into an exciting convergence of two powerful scientific domains: Virtual Reality (VR) and Nanotechnology. The precise and intricate world of Nanotechnology becomes pleasantly navigable with the aid of VR, revolutionizing sectors from healthcare to material science. To fully comprehend this significant development, we journey together through a labyrinth so minuscule that it resides within the realm of atoms and molecules. But fear not, for we paint this journey with apt words and accessible narration. While the topic can be complex, we present it in a way that makes it engaging and digestible for all readers, ensuring you do not need a PhD to appreciate this fascinating intersection of technology. Packed full of insights and forward-thinking perspectives, this report offers a tour into the unseen landscapes of our everyday world. As we delve into "Virtual Reality in Nanotechnology: A Journey into the Minuscule World," prepare yourself for a technological adventure like no other, one that will expand your mind and alter your perception of what's possible.

Chapter 2. Exploring the Convergence: Virtual Reality Meets Nanotechnology

Nanotechnology, the manipulation of matter on an atomic and molecular scale, and Virtual Reality, the simulation of a three-dimensional image or environment that can be interacted with in a seemingly real way, are two exciting and innovative scientific fields. Together, they offer the promise of a new age of technological marvels that could revolutionize everything from medicine to material science.

2.1. The Dawn of Nanotechnology

Nanotechnology, since its inception, has proven to be a game-changer in multiple fields. By enabling the manipulation of individual atoms and molecules, it's reshaping industries and creating immense potential towards a future fraught with unimaginably small and advanced technology.

However, even as fascinating as nanotech is, it's not without its challenges. The nanoscale is so minuscule – a nanometer is one-billionth of a meter – that even conventional microscopes cannot provide clarity in observation. The research in this field has been akin to maneuvering in the dark, with scientists having to rely heavily on computer algorithms and indirect methods to understand nanomaterials' behaviors.

2.2. The Emergence of Virtual Reality

Parallel to the development of nanotechnology, Virtual Reality (VR), once merely the stuff of science fiction, has become a reality within our grasp. VR provides an immersive environment that stimulates our senses to interact with a virtual world. It is a mature technology that has permeated domains ranging from gaming and entertainment to education and healthcare.

One of the key features of VR is it allows us to visualize and interact with scenarios that are either non-existent, hard to access, or highly complex. It gifts us the power to comprehend things that would otherwise remain alien to the human imagination.

2.3. Convergence: A Marriage of Scale and Perception

The intersection of VR and Nanotechnology opens a new horizon of possibilities. The combination aims to address the inaccessibility of the nanoworld by translating the intricate realm into a perceivable virtual space. In other words, VR could allow scientists to 'see' the nano realm.

By creating virtual representations of molecules and structures at the nanoscale, VR can offer an interactive and immersive experience. Such an innovation fulfills dual purposes: aiding research and offering an unprecedented educational tool where students can literally walk around atoms and molecules, deepening their understanding.

2.4. Creating the Infinitesimal Interface: VR in Labs

To envision the impact of VR in nanotech research, imagine scientists donning VR headsets and virtually diving into minuscule landscapes. They can observe atomic structures from multiple angles, conduct experiments, mimic reactions, and visualize results in real-time.

Being able to interact with the nano world in this manner not only offers a unique perspective into the material structure but also pushes the boundaries of understanding atomic behavior. Researchers can spot irregularities, predict outcomes, and adjust experimental parameters more effectively than ever before.

2.5. VR in Nanomedicine: A Promising Partnership

In the field of medicine, the integration of VR and Nanotechnology can manifest advancements that border on the miraculous. With VR, the delivery of nanomaterials inside the human body can be visualized and manipulated with high precision.

Imaging techniques like MRI and CT scans can be translated into interactive 3D models, enabling medical professionals to administer nanoparticles in a precise location. For example, VR could visualize a drugs journey to a cancer cell, empowering personalized care tailored to the patient's own body.

Furthermore, interactive VR platforms can also be used for training purposes, teaching medical professionals how to use nanoscale devices, or demonstrating complex procedures.

2.6. Ethical Considerations and Future Perspectives

Though the possibilities are limitless, and the benefits enormous, we must also consider the ethical implications that this convergence could incur. Ensuring the responsible application of these technologies is crucial since mishandled nanotechnology can potentially be harmful. Similarly, safeguarding a user's experience in the virtual realm carries equal importance.

Looking forward, as VR and Nanotechnology mature and become more intricately connected, their convergence will continue to offer groundbreaking opportunities. These two technologies are set to redefine the boundaries of what we perceive as the interface between the physical and the digital. Their combined force suggests a future where the gulf between the tangible and the simulated is effectively bridged.

In conclusion, the fusion of VR and nanotechnology is leading us into an era where our understanding of the world, its particles, and its processes are poised to expand beyond our current capacity. The journey towards this exciting technological adventure is just beginning, and we are enroute to experiencing a paradigm shift in science and technology as never seen before.

Chapter 3. The Basics of VR and Nanotech: A Gentle Introduction

Before we embark on this fantastic voyage, we must first equip ourselves with the understanding of the two key technologies that make this journey possible: Virtual Reality and Nanotechnology. To comprehend the marvels these technologies present when united, we must individually understand them in their own right.

3.1. Virtual Reality: A Doorway to Immersive Experiences

Imagine being able to scale mountains, walk on alien planets, or navigate the human bloodstream, all while sitting comfortably in your living room. This is the magic of Virtual Reality (VR). It's a technology that constructs immersive digital environments, allowing users to engage in places and experiences outside their physical reach.

The term 'Virtual Reality' might feel very modern, but its origins trace back to 1968 when Ivan Sutherland and Bob Sproull developed the first head-mounted display, The Sword of Damocles. Over time, advancements in the field have led to the development of fully immersive VR systems, combining high-resolution visuals with haptic feedback, giving users a more tangible sense of interaction with the virtual environment.

The backbone of a VR system is its hardware, primarily composed of a Head-Mounted Display (HMD) that offers 3D visual effects, Motion Tracking Systems that captures user movements, and Controllers that allow users to interact with the VR environment.

On the software front, VR developers create comprehensive 3D environments using computer graphics, photorealistic imaging, and a dose of artificial intelligence to ensure a lifelike interaction within the VR world. The software responds to the user's actions, promoting an immersive and realistic experience that transcends the confines of our physical world.

3.2. Nanotechnology: The Power to Manipulate the Tiny

Nanotechnology, as the name suggests, involves working with matter on an incredibly small scale - specifically, at the nanometer level. One nanometer is a billionth of a meter, nearly 10,000 times smaller than the width of a human hair, a scale invisible to even the most powerful optical microscopes.

While challenges are abundant at this scale, they are matched by the remarkable potential for innovation. With devices and structures built at the molecular level, we can unlock capabilities and performances far beyond existing technologies.

Nanotechnology was first conceptualized in 1959 by physicist Richard Feynman in his talk "There's Plenty of Room at the Bottom." Feynman proposed the idea that it should be possible to manipulate individual atoms and molecules to create new materials and miniaturize technology. Today, this vision is a reality.

3.3. The Convergence of VR and Nanotechnology

The integration of VR and Nanotechnology may initially seem unlikely, given their divergent scales of operation. VR primarily exists within human-sized spaces, allowing us to explore virtual environments that reflect our macro-scale perception, whereas

Nanotechnology pushes the limits of our understanding at the atomic level, a world far removed from our daily experience.

Yet, this stark contrast provides precisely the unique opportunity for collaboration. Our inability to naturally perceive and explore the nanoworld is the problem VR is perfectly suited to address. By transforming the molecular landscape into a navigable 3D environment, VR can bring nanotechnology within the reach of our senses.

This convergence has the potential to revolutionize many scientific fields. For instance, biochemists could use VR representations to understand complex proteins structures, leading to significant advancements in drug discovery. Similarly, nanotechnologists could use VR to design and construct microscopic machines or advanced materials at the molecular level.

As we continue this journey, remember that the fusion of VR and Nanotechnology is like a confluence of two mighty rivers, resulting in an enormously potent scientific tool. The promise of this combined technology resides not simply in our ability to investigate the world at an atomic scale but to interact with that world firsthand, all through the power of VR. This integration is more than a marriage of the macro and micro; it is an extraordinary partnership, unlocking a universe of possibilities unimaginable a few decades ago. As our journey into "Virtual Reality in Nanotechnology: A Journey into the Minuscule World" unfolds, our respect and appreciation for these complementary technologies is set to deepen.

Chapter 4. Manipulating the Minuscule: VR in Nanotechnology

Humans have, since the dawn of history, tried to extend their sensory capabilities. From the simple act of venturing into the dark, using fire to illuminate the way, to the invention of telescopes to behold the cosmos, we have innovatively and relentlessly sought ways to transcend our natural limitations. In the quest to understand and manipulate matter at an atomic scale, one could argue we are still at a nascent stage due to limitations in our sensory apparatus. The convergence of Virtual Reality (VR) and Nanotechnology promises a paradigm shift in our ability to interact with this minuscule realm.

4.1. VR in Nanotechnology: A Peak Beneath the Surface

Virtual Reality is a computer-generated simulation of a three-dimensional environment that can be interacted with in a seemingly real or physical way by a person using special electronic equipment, such as a head-mounted display or gloves embedded with sensors. A user in such a VR environment can perform actions, manipulate objects, and react to situations in a manner comparable to what they could do in the real world.

Nanotechnology, on the other hand, is the design, characterization, production, and application of structures, devices, and systems by controlling shape and size at the nanometer scale. A nanometer is one-billionth of a metre, about 1/80,000 of the diameter of a human hair, or ten times the diameter of a hydrogen atom.

When harnessed together, these technologies promise a world where researchers not only observe the nanoworld but also manipulate it, with an intimate 'hands-on' approach that was unimaginable a few decades ago.

4.2. Scaling Down: Seeing the Invisible

Integrating VR with nanotechnology yields a powerful tool for visualizing complex nanostructures and manipulating them. Initially, this involves scaling the nanoscopic up to a size perceivable by human senses. Here, VR plays an instrumental role. We're defying conventional parameters of perception, turning the miniature into the massive.

Creating a VR environment that accurately represents nanostructures involves combining advanced mathematical modeling, molecular simulations, and experimental data from a variety of instruments such as electron microscopes and atomic force microscopes. This shepherds scientists past the age of static pictorial representations, which are subject to misinterpretations, into an interactive realm where they can observe, study, and manipulate atoms and molecules firsthand.

4.3. A Hands-on Approach: The Unseen Tangible

Beyond visualization, the convergence of VR and nanotechnology provides an unprecedented environment for tangible interaction with nanostructures. Sensors attached to specially designed gloves capture the user's hand movements and translates these into the VR environment. These motions can then be scaled down to manipulate individual molecules or atoms within the nanostructure.

The feedback loop this creates is transformative, as it allows scientists to 'feel' the forces as they work with molecules or atoms. Such experiential learning not only fast-tracks researchers' understanding of structures at the nanoscale but also breaks down the barrier of inaccessibility that has accompanied nanoscience.

4.4. Nanomotors and Precision Engineering

Take, for example, the design and operation of nanomotors — tiny machines that can perform tasks at the atomic level. Manipulating these infinitesimal components with traditional tools and techniques is incredibly challenging. However, in a VR setting, a researcher can effectively 'reach in' and nudge, rotate, or even snap pieces together. This kind of meticulous, hands-on approach at the atomic level could lead to the tailoring of molecular motors or precisely constructed nanoscale machines.

4.5. A Revolution in Material Science

The broader ramifications are also noteworthy. The ability for users to virtually interact with and manipulate individual nanostructures, combined with real-time multiscale modeling that feeds back the results instantaneously, could shine a light on unexplored corridors of material science. We might craft materials with specific traits — like flexibility, strength, or conductivity — by manipulating their atomic structure, straight from our virtual interfaces.

4.6. Biomedical Applications: Healing Hands

The crossover of VR and nanotechnology isn't strictly limited to the world of physics and material science. A significant leap forward is also envisioned in the biomedical sector. The design and implementation of nanoscale drug delivery systems could be accomplished with increased precision — doctors might design and virtually pilot nanoparticle vessels to deliver drugs to precise locations within the human body.

Indeed, VR could transform the way we uncover the secrets written in the language of life itself by allowing a more tactile exploration of DNA strands. Unraveling, twisting, and piecing together these building blocks of life with our virtual hands could lead to remarkable new insights into genetic disorders and more efficient methods for gene editing.

The marriage of VR and Nanotechnology is an exciting cross-disciplinary scientific dialogue, one that promises to open up the world beneath the world. The ability to manipulate the minuscule facets of reality at an atomic level gives us a profound new toolset with which we can advance our understanding of the natural world and our place within it. This evolving discourse, bridging the realms of the vast and the infinitesimal, marks just the beginning of human interaction with the nano realm on such an intimate level. The smallest of scales might just usher in the most significant possibilities.

Chapter 5. Healthcare Revolution: Nanobots Guided by VR

Nanotechnology, ushering in an era of unprecedented possibilities, is central to a suite of groundbreaking healthcare innovations. As it melds with Virtual Reality (VR), the vista of its actualization dramatically expands, enhancing diagnosis, therapy, and even the manner in which we perform surgeries.

5.1. Paradigms of Nanotechnology and VR in Healthcare

To appreciate the extent of this intersect, it is essential to understand the individual modalities of both Nanotechnology and VR in healthcare. Nanotechnology involves the manipulation of matter at an atomic, molecular, and supramolecular scale, typically less than 100 nanometers in size. In healthcare, nanotechnology is proving instrumental in domains such as drug delivery, diagnostics, implant materials, and even fighting cancer.

VR, on the other hand, involves the creation of computer-simulated environments that replicate an entity's presence in real or imagined worlds. In healthcare, VR is gaining traction in areas such as pain management, exposure therapy, stroke rehabilitation, and surgical training and planning.

5.2. Nanobots and VR: The Symbiosis

When nanotechnology and VR collide, it unlocks new frontiers, a noteworthy one being the use of VR to navigate and control nanobots at a cellular or molecular level within the human body. Nanobots, tiny man-made machines, operate at a nanoscale, capable of carrying out complex tasks. The potential for medicine is unlimited, from targeted drug delivery to precise surgery, and even repairing at a cellular level.

5.3. Nanobots in Drug Delivery

The therapeutic potential of drugs often becomes limited due to unfavorable physicochemical properties, targeting inefficiencies, low bioavailability, or systemic side effects. Nanobots, with their ability for pinpoint precision delivery of drugs, revolutionize this arena.

One can compare nanobots to a selective delivery system, conveying drugs precisely to the desired location, and at the correct dosage and timing. This precision reduces side effects and increases the efficacy of the drugs by ensuring they only reach the targeted cells. Minimizing collateral damage, nanobots provide a new prognosis for conditions previously rendered hopeless. VR assists in mapping this path of delivery, enabling doctors or surgeons to visually invoke and monitor these journeys in real-time.

5.4. Nanobots in Surgery and Disease Treatment

In the realm of surgery, nanobots' ability to manipulate substances atom by atom brings a revolution. Surgeons can guide nanobots to perform complex tasks such as removing plaque from blood vessels, repairing cells, and even eradicating cancer cells. Surgeons pilot these nanobots through VR operating consoles that are projected as three-dimensional models. Via haptic feedback mechanisms, the surgeon can 'feel' the internal structure of the patient, suggesting an unrivalled precision level.

In cancer treatment, nanobots have shown promise in destroying tumors without harming healthy tissue. A research team from Arizona State University and the National Center for Nanoscience and Technology of the Chinese Academy of Sciences developed nanobots from DNA folded in origami style. Programmed to locate tumors, these nanobots cut off their blood supply, causing them to shrink and die. VR adds a significant dimension of control and visibility to these promising procedures.

5.5. Nanobots in Therapy

Nanotechnology also provides potential for regenerative medicine. The capability of nanobots to intervene and repair at a cellular level is a cardinal shift from traditional therapeutic interventions. It could potentially help patients suffering from issues such as neuronal damage in Alzheimer's or Parkinson's. VR pathways allow for precise navigation and intervention.

5.6. The Challenges Ahead

While the merger of VR and nanotechnology promises unexplored territories, it doesn't come without challenges. Privacy concerns, cyber threats, potential toxicity, long-term effects of nanobots, and lack of regulation can be roadblocks to this exciting convergence. It is essential to have robust legislation to ensure the ethical use of this technology.

The convergence of VR and nanotechnology is not a mere fanciful adumbration of science and technology but a palpable reality that can redefine medical care. It transcends traditional barriers of medicine, offering hope for otherwise elusive treatments. With nanobots guided by VR, we stand on the cusp of a healthcare revolution. However, it becomes paramount to tread this path thoughtfully, ensuring we balance the nurturing of this innovation with ethical considerations.

Chapter 6. Material Science Redefined: The Small-Scale Architects

Few realms could benefit more profoundly from the marriage of Virtual Reality (VR) and Nanotechnology than the sphere of material science. These small-scale architects are redefining the way we understand the world and the products we create, creating a seismic shift in our scientific capabilities.

6.1. The Nano Scale World

So, what do we mean by the term "nanoscale"? A nanometer (nm) is one billionth of a meter, and the nanoscale ranges up to 100 nm. This size is roughly 100,000 times smaller than the diameter of a human hair. It is in this realm where the fundamental building blocks of our world assemble and shape an array of marvels. To interact with and understand this nanoscale world better, we need a tool that can traverse its infinitesimal landscape. This is where VR comes into play, providing an interface capable of simulating the nanoscale milieu in intricate detail.

6.2. Virtual Reality as a Tool in Material Science

VR enhances the interaction between humans and nanoscale phenomena by presenting a three-dimensional representation that, while enormous in human terms, remains faithful to the structures and behaviors found at the nanoscale. It allows material scientists to "walk" through the atomic lattices of metals, "see" the charge distribution in a molecule, and even "manipulate" individual atoms.

Virtual Reality, acting as a sensory enhancement device, magnifies the imperceptible, transforming the small-scale architects of nanotechnology into entities we can intuitively comprehend and manage. Beyond providing a riveting sci-fi experience, VR aids the construction, design, and understanding of engineered nanostructures.

6.3. Improving Atomic Understanding

For a scientist, being able to observe atomic interactions and movements in real time is priceless. With VR, we are getting closer and closer to this previously unattainable goal.

Revolutionizing theoretical material science, VR interfaces can now generate real-time simulations of atomic and molecular dynamics. Scientists can effortlessly observe and track the motion, interaction, and evolution of individual atoms. These visualizations provide critical insights about how materials form and behave on the atomic scale, opening new frontiers for the design of meta-materials and nanostructures.

6.4. Nanoscale Manufacturing

In addition to observing, VR coupled with nanotechnology brings an exciting prospect: Nanoscale manufacturing. With appropriate tools in a virtual environment, scientists can organize and manipulate atoms and molecules interactively. Building structures grain by grain, this technique is akin to atomic 3D printing, revolutionizing material manufacturing as we know it. Pioneering research in molecular dynamics and quantum physics, coupled with VR's visualization prowess, propels the idea of "materials-by-design" from the realm of concept into reality.

6.5. Revolutionizing Material Properties

The potential of nanoscale manipulation through VR is not limited to creating structures. By maneuvering atoms and molecules, one achieves a deep understanding of their dynamic properties and relationships. Consequently, scientists can discover and devise ingenious methods to alter material properties, such as strength, elasticity, conductivity, and chemical reactivity. This small-scale, hands-on exploration offers a powerful connection between the invisible nanoworld and the macroscopic properties of materials, redefining conventional wisdom about how things work.

6.6. Unseen Challenges and Unprecedented Prospects

Despite the promise, the reality is that the marriage of VR and nanotechnology is still in its nascent stage. The larger challenges lie in achieving sub-atomic resolution and compatibility between VR and experimental data. But as computational capabilities and VR technologies continue to progress, these issues are expected to be surmounted, opening the path for a deeper integration of VR into nanoscience.

The convergence of VR and nanotechnology stands to redefine the field of material science. As we advance our exploration of the nano world, harnessing VR's power to visualize, comprehend, and manipulate this unseen landscape, we are truly stepping into a new era of scientific discovery and technological innovation.

Chapter 7. Education Paradigm Shift: Learning at the Nano Level with VR

In crafting a comprehensive report, we first examine the unfolding shift in education paradigms through the lens of Virtual Reality and Nanotechnology. To put these advancements in context, we reflect on traditional learning methods, illustrating how they often fall short when explaining abstract or hard-to-grasp concepts. Hand-drawn diagrams and textbook explanations are valuable resources, but there are certain complexities they can't simplistically replicate or empathetically communicate, such as the behaviors and interactions at the nano level. This is where the convergence of VR and Nanotechnology becomes particularly transformative – welcome to the exciting era of immersive, nano-scale learning.

7.1. Old vs. New: From Chalkboard to Nano-Simulator

Historically, teaching nanotechnology has been a challenge due to its inherent complexity and abstract nature. For decades, we've relied on textbook diagrams, mathematical formulas, and lengthy verbal explanations to unpack these microscopic phenomena. However, it's clear that these once-effective tools are now, quite literally, coming up short. Imagine the gap between reading about the Grand Canyon and actually standing at its edge; a similar analogy can be drawn in the context of nano-scale education.

Now, picture a classroom where textbooks are replaced with VR headsets, chalkboards exchanged for nano-simulators. As students dive into the navigation and manipulation of atomic structures, these immersive tools enable them to visually perceive, interact with, and alter an atom's structure, offering a realistic and immediate comprehension of nanoscience principles.

7.2. Interactive Learning: VR as Nanotechnology's Roadmap

Virtual Reality offers a unique approach to nanotechnology education, making the unseen world visible. VR provides an interactive, immersive experience where learners explore and manipulate nanostructures in three-dimensional space. Instead of merely reading about atomic interactions, students can witness atoms merging, bonding, and transitioning in real time.

The immersion achieved through VR creates a sense of spatial awareness, enabling learners to understand the scale, proportions, and relationships between nano-sized particles better. With VR headsets, learners can adjust the scale from a human-sized environment down to the nano level, getting a true appreciation of the minute scale of atoms and molecules. This hands-on, responsive learning experience is a radical departure from conventional teaching methods, but one that offers tremendous potential for effective, engaging education.

7.3. Beyond Visualisation: Haptic Feedback in VR Nanoscience

Beyond spatial and visual immersion, developments in haptic technology now allow learners to 'feel' the nanoscale world. Haptic feedback devices connected to VR systems provide tactile sensations that synchronize with the learners' actions in the virtual environment. Combining haptic feedback with VR enhances the learning process, making it a multi-sensory experience. This synchronistic approach creates deeper cognitive connections, increasing knowledge retention.

For instance, students can 'feel' the force of attraction between particles or the effect of magnetic fields at the nano scale. Such an approach radically improves the cognitive learning process, delivering a persuasive sense of 'presence' within the VR environment that no chalk-and-board education could ever achieve.

7.4. Enhanced Collaboration: Learning in Unison

The synergy between VR and Nanotechnology also fosters collaboration. Students can simultaneously inhabit the same virtual nano environment, experiencing real-time interactions and changes, and discussing their observations and hypotheses together. The nano world, once confined to individual imaginations based on textual descriptions and static diagrams, has now become a shared, dynamic learning realm.

Virtual collaborative environments permit rich, shared experiences, fostering peer learning, and enhancing critical thinking skills. They provide an engaging, context-rich landscape in which educators can guide students in exploring nanoscale principles, experimenting with molecular structures, and generating new scientific inquiries.

7.5. Conclusion

The fusion of VR and Nanotechnology opens the doors to a dynamic, immersive educational paradigm that is likely to transform nano education substantially. It enables concepts that were once abstract and inaccessible to become tangible, visible, and understandable, transforming the classroom into an engaging, active learning environment.

We now stand on the precipice of a dramatic shift in the way we teach and learn about the world at the nano level. A world where the complexities and intricacies of atoms and molecules are no longer barriers to learning, but rather bridges to greater understanding. This is the paradigm shift that VR brings to nanotechnology education, marking the dawn of a new era in the science of learning. As we move forward, we must embrace this shift and explore the myriad possibilities it opens for the future of education.

While education represents just one application of VR in nanotechnology, the potential applications span far beyond, infiltrating various sectors from healthcare to material science. As we continue to delve into other exciting areas, we witness the profound impact of this powerful convergence and how it's revolutionizing our everyday world.

What follows in the sections to come is a wealth of revolutionary perspectives and insights garnered from the frontier of VR and nanotechnological convergence. Journey forth, reader, equipped with this comprehensive backdrop of the grand classroom transformation, a pivotal piece in our overall narrative: "Virtual Reality in Nanotechnology: A Journey into the Minuscule World."

Chapter 8. Virtual Ethics: Responsible Innovation at the Nano Scale

As humanity plumbs the depths of the microscopic universe and conjures technologies from the realm of atoms and molecules, it's imperative that we pause for a moment to address the ethical implications of these advancements as well.

8.1. Responsibility in Innovation

Innovations at the nanoscale bear tremendous potential to revolutionize every sector of our society. From cancer-fighting 'nano-bots' destined to traverse our bodies to the creation of smarter materials and cleaner energy, the possibilities seem endless. However, as we continue to innovate, we must be mindful of our moral responsibility to do so safely, ethically, and sustainably.

Every technological transformation carries within it not just the seed of human progression, but the prospect of harm and consequence as well. For instance, the creation of more effective medicines or stronger materials must not compromise patient privacy or lead to a disparity in resource distribution. As responsible innovators, it's crucial to align our decisions with the fundamental principles of equity, fairness, and respect for autonomy.

8.2. Anticipating and Mitifying Risks

At this juncture, a crucial aspect of responsible innovation is the anticipation of ethical, social, and environmental risks. These potential risks can be from nano-material contamination, privacy intrusion by microscopic surveillance devices, or misuse of nanotechnologies in ways that could violate human rights or civil liberties. Mitigation strategies include proactive risk assessment, public engagement, regulatory oversight, and investment in targeted research to understand potential risks better.

Communication plays an integral component of this process, ensuring that everyone – from policymakers to the public – understands the potential impacts of nanotechnology. It encourages informed decision-making and facilitates the formation of regulations that align with societal values and expectations.

8.3. Public Engagement and Democratic Decision-Making

Public involvement in decision-making about nanotechnology is invaluable. Lay perspectives can offer insights that experts may overlook, particularly regarding non-technical factors such as societal acceptance and ethical concerns. Meaningful public engagement can take various forms, from town hall meetings and citizens' juries, to online consultations and surveys.

Such democratic decision-making processes should be designed to represent all sectors of society. This process will ensure equity and fairness in the development and distribution of nanotechnologies, preventing the concentration of benefits within a select group and distributing the risk fairly among all stakeholders involved.

8.4. Regulatory Issues and Global Governance

Building a regulatory consensus on nanotechnology across different countries is critical. As nanotechnology transcends national borders, its regulation also requires international coordination. The global governance of nanotechnology should be based on principles of transparency, accountability, and public justification. Such governance should also foster international partnerships to address shared challenges and promote equitable access to nanotechnology globally.

This robust regulatory framework would assure the public of the safety and effectiveness of nanotechnologies while fostering innovation and market confidence. Incorporation of a "responsive regulation" approach, having tools and processes for real-time adaptation, is especially useful when dealing with emergent technologies like nanotechnology.

8.5. Ethics in Technological Development

Nanotechnologies, as with all technologies, can have unanticipated effects. The ethical responsibility in technological development demands us to accept and respond to these facets responsibly. Prioritizing ethical considerations in the foresight of technological development could arguably prevent unnecessary harms or misuse of technology.

The development of ethical frameworks for the governance of nanotechnologies will be a cornerstone for the maturation of this field. It is an ongoing journey, fostering conversations between scientists, ethicists, and society as a whole to ensure the ethical implications of nanotechnologies are thoughtfully evaluated and addressed.

Principles like the precautionary principle, advocating for acting in the face of uncertainty to avoid harm, and the proactionary principle, encouraging the pursuit of beneficial applications of technology while controlling the harms, could serve as guides in creating these ethical frameworks.

The study of nanoethics encompasses all these concepts and more. It widens our lens, enabling a broader understanding of nanotechnology's risks, benefits, moral implications, and societal impacts.

In conclusion, as we push the boundaries of science and technology, ethics must be at the heart of all advances. As we tether ourselves more closely to the realm of nanotech, it's crucial that we ensure our pursuit of innovation remains rooted in the principles of responsibility, safety, equity, and justice. In this way, we will truly harness the immense potentials of nanotechnology, creating a future in which technology not only propels us forward but also makes us better.

Chapter 9. Future Forecast: Glimpses of Tomorrow's Nano-VR World

The future unfolds as an appealing amalgamation of advances in nanotechnology and virtual reality (VR). They usher in an epoch where the minuscule meets the immersive, crafting a potential that is expansive and far-reaching. In our examination of this futuristic vista, we explore key areas such as the potentials in healthcare, material science, education, and the underlying challenges.

9.1. Health: Healing with Precision

Tomorrow's healthcare landscape bodes promising prospects for Nano-VR. Physicians and researchers could delve into the human body at an atomic scale, exploring, diagnosing, and even healing with unmatched precision.

Virtual reality serves as a road into the organic labyrinths of our bodies, navigating through blood vessels, and rendering vivid explorations of cellular structures. Therapies could become minutely targeted, reducing undesired side effects and increasing efficacy of treatments. With Nano-VR, we might see the advent of 'smart drugs' that can be guided to specific locations, bearing precise doses of medication, with VR acting as the real-time monitoring and remote controlling tool.

In medical education, no longer will students dissect cadavers, learning through trial and error. The Nano-VR interface could be providing them with a hands-on experience deep into the human system, offering real-time feedback and cases that may span from common ailments to rare disease studies.

9.2. Material Science: Crafting from the Atomic Up

In the realm of material science, Nano-VR prepares to fuel a revolution. The ability to interact with individual atoms and molecules could unlock the potential to craft materials at a granular level. Materials could be designed with bespoke attributes, like ultra-strength lightweight alloys, self-healing materials, and more.

Imagine architects, engineers, and designers working together in a shared VR environment to craft materials atom by atom—then testing their physical properties without investing resources in creating a physical prototype. This level of intimate interaction and the capacity to construct and deconstruct at a nanoscale could be the new norm in the material designing industry.

9.3. Education: Learning Through Experience

VR's immersive element, combined with detailed nanoscale environments, could make learning more experiential. Imagine chemistry students not simply reading about reactions, but navigating through them at an atomic level, watching bonds form and break, or physics students witnessing the quantum world's oddities firsthand.

The physical laws governing reality are vastly different at nanoscales—here, quantum mechanics holds sway. The Nano-VR combination would offer a glimpse into this reality, transforming abstract concepts into educational landscapes and creating a deeper understanding.

9.4. Overcoming Challenges: Nurturing the Nano-VR Convergence

While the potential benefits of Nano-VR are tremendous, challenges exist that need to be overcome. Developing nanoscale models with such detail and precision that they reflect reality is a daunting task.

Creating an interface to control and interact with atoms remotely in a VR environment also poses sizeable hurdles. Safety measures need to be designed, considering the implications of misusing such powerful technology. Ensuring equitable access to these advancements is another issue that needs to be addressed.

9.5. A Vision of the Nano-VR Future

As we look ahead at the future of Nano-VR, we see an interconnected world where virtual reality and nanotechnology blur the lines between digital and physical. The myriad of possibilities that this technology could spawn is undoubtedly exciting—ranging from molecular artworks to decoding the complexities of the universe.

However, as with any technology, perhaps what is most important is how we wield it. Nano-VR holds the potential to unlock a myriad of wonders within the nano cosmos and enrich our understanding of the world. In the right hands and driven with ethical considerations, it offers a future brimming with innovation and advancement. Embracing this technological symphony can importantly transform our existence, and this is only a glimpse into tomorrow's Nano-VR world.

Chapter 10. Real World Nano-VR Applications: Small Steps, Giant Leaps

As breathtaking as theoretical presentations may appear, nothing quite validates the potency of two converging technologies quite like their real-world applications. In this instance, it is the fascinating fusion of Virtual Reality (VR) and nanotechnology that's shaping an unprecedented trajectory of innovation and progress. Renowned for their individual capacities, VR's simulation prowess and nanotechnology's manipulation of tiny elements bring about a deluge of opportunities when intertwined. From remapping healthcare sagas to redefining the contours of material design, the plane of technological possibility has been thrust into exhilarating new dimensions.

10.1. Virtual Reality in Healthcare: Nanotechnology's New Eyesight

The radical intersection of VR and nanotechnology, both are playing transformative roles in the healthcare sphere. Scientists are leveraging VR to study nanoscale biological phenomena, with promising implications for disease analysis and drug discovery.

By utilizing VR, researchers can immerse themselves in a 3D, simulated environment to interact with complex nanostructures. This method offers a more comprehensive, almost tactile experience that no traditional 2D projection can bestow. As a result, it fosters a deeper understanding of intricate biological machinations and accelerates the development of tailored nanoscale solutions.

For instance, scientists at the Stanford Nano Shared Facilities have applied VR to visualize and manipulate atomic structures, augmenting their work in studying the properties of various materials. Additionally, VR simulations have been significant in understanding nano-carriers, the tiny particles that deliver drugs to targeted sites in the body.

10.2. Nano-Machines and Smart Materials

Beyond healthcare, VR combined with nanotechnology is making waves in the territory of smart materials and nanomachines. Mimicking nature's designs at an atomic scale often leads to incredibly efficient solutions. Spider silk's strength, butterfly wing's vibrant colors - these are nano-engineered miracles. Nanotechnologists wish to recreate such miracles, for instance, developing super-strong materials or vibration absorbing surfaces.

However, designing at an atomic scale is no simple task. Aided by VR, scientists work within a virtually simulated nano world, manipulating individual atoms and molecules like building blocks. It's this VR-enabled design process that birthed nanomachines – nano entities capable of performing tasks at the molecular level. These nanomachines are paving the way for a future where we can engineer materials possessing self-healing properties or design smart sensors on a nanoscale.

10.3. VR Aiding Nanotechnology in Education

The possibilities engendered by a fusion of VR and nanotechnology aren't just limited to laboratory developments. It permeates into the classroom as well, creating a significant impact on education. Understanding constructs at a nanoscale can, understandably, be challenging for students. Concepts that deal with one billionth of a meter are difficult to visualize and even more challenging to relate to real-world applications.

Here, VR becomes a useful tool. By simulating the nanoworld in a 3D, interactive environment, abstract notions assume a tangible form. VR experiences, such as NanoSimbox, enable students to play, experiment, and interact with atomic and molecular structures, fostering their understanding of nanoscience. VR is not just a pedagogical tool but a method to inspire the next generation of nano scientists.

10.4. A Glimpse into the Future

Nanotechnology combined with VR carries us into a realm where atoms can be seen and manipulated, where abstract scientific concepts become immersive experiences, and where students, researchers, and scientists can delve first-hand into the minuscule world. Even though still in its nascent stage, it's apparent that the fusion of VR and nanotechnology harbors untold opportunities. This grandeur journey into the world's tiniest parts may one day enable us to build solutions to the world's most significant challenges.

In conclusion, the merger of VR and nanotech looks set to redefine processes across various sectors, riveting all eyes firmly on the unfolding nano-VR revolution. The burgeoning industry boasts immense potential yet sees itself at the threshold of discoveries. We may not know the future implications fully, but we certainly are set to witness colossal strides in technology and innovation, as VR and nanotechnology unite to create small steps with giant leaps.

Chapter 11. The Road Ahead: Challenges and Opportunities in Nano-VR

As we strive to harness the full scope of Nano-VR—the exciting intersection of nanotechnology and virtual reality—diligently we encounter both formidable challenges and enthralling opportunities. Know however that the intent of discussing these is not to discourage or dispirit, but to fortify our understanding and prepare for the fascinating road that stretches ahead in this endeavor.

11.1. The Wayward Complexity of Nanoscale Structures

To start, let's consider a significant challenge: the complexity of nanostructures. The natural world is replete with complex systems that operate on a scale beyond our usual perception. Viewing and understanding these elements at the nanoscale can be daunting, as our perceptions and intuitions, honed on macroscopic scales, fail to equip us to grasp the intricacies of these minuscule structures.

However, with the application of VR, we can now "zoom in" and traverse these microscopic landscapes with newfound freedom. For instance, we can virtually "walk" along the convoluted ribbons of proteins or glide alongside the surface of a microchip, turning otherwise abstract concepts into relatable visual experiences. The challenge lies in accurately modeling these complex structures. It is essential to ensure scientific accuracy while translating them into a virtual world for further exploration.

11.2. The Challenges of Entering the Quantum Realm

A step beyond lies the quantum realm. Nanotechnology often calls for the manipulation of individual atoms and molecules, which requires a plunge into quantum mechanics. Here, conventional laws of physics seem to be suspended, and the probabilistic nature of particle behavior reigns supreme. To understand this unpredictable realm and interpret it in a VR environment is a momentous task, as quantum physics is counterintuitive to our everyday lived experiences.

Nonetheless, this challenge presents an opportunity. By harnessing the immersive power of VR, we can develop virtual laboratories where quantum phenomena can be studied and tested on demand. With future advancements, we might even build quantum teleportation stations or quantum computing centers in a VR setting where individuals can learn, experiment, and innovate.

11.3. Accessibility, Usability and Skills Gap

As with any field of technology, the ingenuity and breakthroughs only make a substantial difference if they are accessible and usable to a broad audience. Currently, VR is not universally accessible. High costs, limited outreach, and required skills pose obstacles to the democratisation of VR. Hence, bringing Nano-VR to classrooms, laboratories, and industries worldwide faces a logistical challenge.

However, this challenge brings the opportunity to innovate in cost-effective VR solutions and simplified interface designs. A focus on improving accessibility and usability of VR technology can foster democratization, bringing the nano-world within reach of budding scientists, innovators, and curious minds around the globe.

11.4. Juggling Accuracy and Real-time Interactivity

A subtle but crucial challenge is striking a balance between scientific accuracy and real-time interactivity in the Nano-VR realm. While presenting nanoscale structures and phenomena, maintaining a high degree of accuracy is paramount. On the other spectrum, VR's power lies in its immersive real-time interactivity. To optimize both without compromising either is a complex task.

In response, this challenge paves the way for the evolution of next-generation computational solutions and algorithms that would allow higher accuracy without compromising real-time responses. Advanced artificial intelligence (AI) and machine learning (ML) algorithms could be instrumental in achieving this harmony, hence opening up a new area of study and experimentation.

11.5. Ethical and Security Considerations

Nanotech and VR both have their inherent ethical implications and security concerns. For instance, with VR's capacity to simulate reality, there are issues surrounding trust, privacy, and authenticity. Nanotech, with its ability to manipulate substances at atomic levels, poses questions around safety, unforeseen implications, and potential misuse.

In turn, this challenge fuels the need for a robust and globally agreed ethical framework. It stresses the importance of world-wide discussion and consensus-building on the ethical use of these technologies. Encrypting data to ensure privacy, securing VR platforms against misuse, and fostering responsible innovation in nanotechnology should be on the agenda.

The challenges that currently face the convergence of VR and nanotechnology are, undoubtedly, formidable. But as with any great scientific endeavor, the greatest challenges come with the most thrilling opportunities. As we see more advancements and breakthroughs in Nano-VR, the landscape will undoubtedly alter, offering us an unprecedented view into the realms currently beyond our grasp. Nevertheless, a continuous cycle of learning and iterating will bring us closer to turning the incredible potential of Nano-VR into groundbreaking realities.

As with any potent fusion of technologies, Nano-VR bears the potential to revolutionize our understanding of the world. From education to healthcare, material science to renewable energy, the prospects are seemingly endless. However, success lies in not only appreciating the opportunities at hand but also, acknowledging, and diligently addressing the challenges on the road ahead. After all, the most enlightening journeys often meander through the most challenging landscapes. The tale of Nano-VR promises to be one of such unique and mesmerizing journeys.